M000032700

YOU ARE MY VOICE

HOW LOVE'S VOICE NEVER DIES

Lisa Kolias Cooper

To Sue,
Love Never
dies!

Lisa

BIGCHAIR
PUBLISHING

YOU ARE MY VOICE
Lisa Kolias Cooper

Second Edition

Big Chair Publishing
6709 W 119th St. No. 444
Overland Park, KS 66209

Print: ISBN: 978-0-9960800-3-3

10 9   8   7   6   5   4   3   2   1

Printed in the United States of America

youaremyvoice.com

CONTENTS

HER VOICE, MY SIGNS ... 85

ONE MORE BLUE JAY SIGN ... 118

A Nest For You

To my mother, Eleanor,
for sharing her voice
of love, even after death.

To my daughter,
so that she will never forget that
love's voice never dies.

ACKNOWLEDGMENTS

Gratitude to my Book Angel, Barbara Unell,
whose writing and publishing experience,
along with a dear friendship,
illuminated my writing journey.

Blessings to my Earth Angel,
Ruby Scott Meyers, who shared in the spiritual
journey of my mother and me, and provided
years of encouragement for me to follow
my heart and pursue my writing dream.

Love to my husband, daughter, and father,
who watched and listened,
as this book was born.

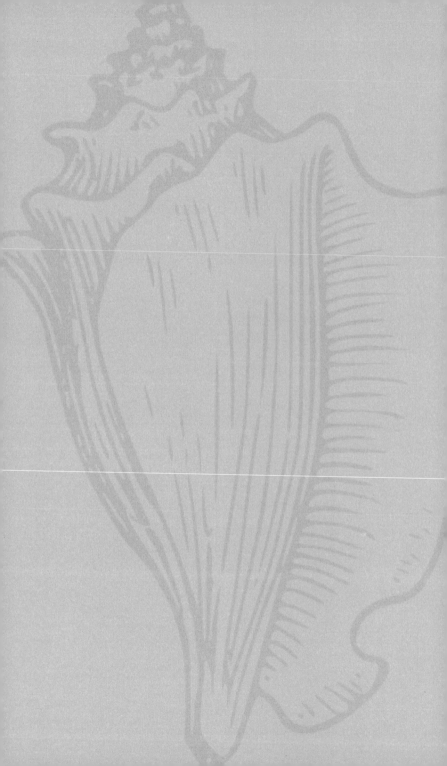

"Although I've left the physical world,
you can hear my voice, if you listen with
your heart and know that I am near."

ELEANOR KOLIAS

Growing up, I shared a special bond with my mother, Eleanor Kolias. She was my rock and sturdy foundation, as I traversed the ups and downs of childhood, teenage years and college independence. As I started a career and moved away from my hometown, our relationship evolved into one of best friends. There wasn't much we didn't share. Even across the miles, her wisdom and unconditional love helped me become the woman I am today.

Her zest for life, hearty laugh and love of nature helped shape my perspectives, as I developed and defined my priorities as an adult. Her ability to relax and restore her spirit allowed me to better understand the notion of "human being" versus "human doing" before the term was ever popular. Most importantly, being my mother's daughter enabled me to learn how to mother and how to love.

With time, came the inevitable parent-child role reversal, where the tables began to turn. It was my turn to be her rock and support. It was my turn to listen, plan and help her navigate aging and an eventual fall from good health.

Shortly after my mother passed on, I began sifting through her belongings. Among her clothes and random knick-knacks, a common theme emerged. I picked up the neatly folded T-shirts from beach vacations, the sunny beach photo of the two of us in a frame made of tiny white shells now faded with time, and the jars of special shells we both had collected on the beach together. I remembered how we had recollected those trips as she lay dying. I now heard her voice in my head:

"Just as the shell leaves the ocean, we leave our physical bodies behind. But if you hold the shell to your ear and listen closely, you'll still hear the waves, even though the shell is far from its ocean home. Although I've left the physical world, you can hear my voice, if you listen with your heart and know that I am near."

⟨⟨⟨∞⟩⟩⟩

Just as my mother had predicted, when I opened my heart, I started receiving vivid Dreams and frequent Signs from her. These helped me believe, without a doubt, that she was not only out of pain and healed, but also an active participant in my life. I knew that the Dreams and Signs were real. The universal synchronicity was too perfect to discount. The inner voice words were too real to forget. And from these experiences, I discovered that after a physical death, there's no pain, but there are plentiful seafood buffets and boat rides into the bay. There are no limits, no worries, no fear and most importantly, only love.

Soon, I began recording my Dreams and writing about the Signs, with the intention of helping others understand that our deceased loved ones are with us in Spirit. I read my stories aloud to a good friend and mentor, sharing my hope that my writing might offer help and solace to people, as they coped with the loss of a loved one.

As we walked out of the local coffee shop together on one of these occasions, a bright shiny object on the ground caught my eye. Right at my feet was a shiny penny from Heaven, and a penny for my thoughts to share with you. May you find that they open your heart and feed your soul!

A New
Beginning

*"To live in hearts we leave
behind is not to die."*

THOMAS CAMPBELL

My Grandmother's Visit

On the fourth day of my mother's hospital stay, I woke before the break of dawn and headed as quickly as possible to see her.

When I walked into her room, she was sitting up in bed, smiling happily and chatting about her beloved cat, Misty. Patting the side of her bed, she was saying, "Here Misty, come sit with me."

It was as if she was in another world, chatting, smiling, oblivious to the pain, happy to see me, yet not fully present. At the time, I described her mental state as "euphoric" and confirmed the medications she was receiving via IV with her nurse. I learned that only strong antibiotics to fight the nasty bacterial infection (MRSA*) and fluids were traveling through her body now. No more narcotics that could trigger this euphoric state were present.

I stood by her bedside and tried to take in her odd, yet joyful tone. She explained that she had been "working on her life story" and had so many more memories to remember. She went on to tell me that my grandmother, her mother, had been in her room to visit today and had told her that "everything was working out as planned and not to worry".

My dear grandmother had passed on in 1985, but my mother and I had always felt her closeness since her passing. This time, however, my mother could see her clearly and was reassured that she was healing by her presence. In fact, she went on to tell me that "Nana" was behind me now!

That particular day was my grandmother's birthday, October 1st, so I told my mother to wish her a happy birthday from me. We had always found it funny that my grandmother and President Jimmy Carter had the same day of birth. We laughed about that again that day.

I was certain that my mother was now in two worlds: One world, where I was standing in her hospital room longing for her to heal and return to her "normal" life, and another world where my deceased grandmother was present as she worked on her life story, with no evidence of sickness.

I knew that on her fourth day of this last hospital stay, my grandmother's "arrival" was a sign that soon she would be escorted home, leaving her family behind.

*MRSA
– Health care associated MRSA (HA-MRSA) Methicillin-resistant Staphylococcus aureus.

DNR Bracelet

As the day wore on, my mother's condition worsened. The physician explained that if we didn't approve the DNR (Do Not Resuscitate) Order, the following would occur: My mother's vitals would start tracking down, and a team of nurses and doctors would rush in to try and resuscitate her via chest compressions. If she survived, kidney dialysis would be a necessity, since the MRSA infection had already wreaked havoc on her kidneys and infiltrated her bloodstream. Then, a subsequent spine surgery would be required to wipe out the infection contracted from the first surgery. She would likely never return home, but would live in an assisted living facility, unable to walk.

Instinctively, I knew that she wanted to fight the infection, but my intuition told me that the road ahead would be more than she would want or could handle in so many ways. To live in pain and neither be able to take care of herself nor be home with her husband, was a scenario that I knew she would have opposed. In fact, I remembered specific discussions we'd had years earlier surrounding end-of-life care, in which I promised her that I would never "keep her alive" in any circumstance.

Less than three weeks before, she had undergone a routine surgical procedure to relieve her horrible back pain. I now recalled the chat that we had shared before her surgery. She had reminded me to "be her voice", if for some reason she couldn't communicate her final health wishes. At the time, we had both laughed at the oddity of her request, in light of the simple procedure.

Remembering those talks of the past, along with the facts that her physicians and specialists were stating now, I knew whole-heartedly that giving the DNR Order was exactly what she would have wanted me to do.

Decisively, I approved the DNR bracelet. At that moment, I became "her voice", a reality that I never dreamed would actually come to pass.

Last Weekend

Even though we had approved the DNR Order, her medical team of specialists recommended a move to the Intensive Care Unit (ICU) for consistent monitoring, as now her condition had dramatically worsened. My father and I adorned the gloves, mask and robe, as we entered her ICU room. Her room was light and so much nicer than the previous one, with a large window. The sun streamed in on that gorgeous October day, the kind of perfect autumn day that we used to love. The ICU nurses were caring and kind, and had time to listen and talk. They listened as I talked about the special closeness that my mother and I shared and the many years of marriage that she enjoyed with my father.

A dear friend came by with coffee and food for my father and me, and a few of my mother's friends stopped in to say good-bye in their own way. By now, we all knew that physical death was near. My mother's disposition was now very peaceful. Although she wasn't speaking, I knew in my heart that she could hear.

My father and I sat by her bedside all day and well into the night. As he held one hand and I held the other, we talked about the wonderful times we had shared as a family. I thanked her for all she'd done for me and for being my mother. Occasionally, she would squeeze my hand to let me know that she heard me and loved me, too.

I recounted some of our vacations and the spiritual quests we'd taken, just the two of us, over the years. On one particular trip to Santa Fe, New Mexico, we had discovered a wonderful bookstore where we sat for hours combing the shelves. She squeezed my hand as I talked about that particular day, and I knew that she was remembering that trip, too.

As I recalled that trip and special bookstore, a particular book, titled *Emmanuel's Book*, that contained advice about dealing with death, came to mind. One memorable line read: "Death is like taking off a tight shoe."

I repeated that line to her now, somehow knowing that it needed to be shared aloud. Immediately, she squeezed my hand as hard as she could. I'm not certain if she understood at that point that she was going to die, based on the facts and her serious medical condition. But I followed my intuition and felt that she needed me to share these thoughts to help her on her journey, whether she stayed on Earth or moved on. Her body had become a tight shoe filled with pain and infection. If death was like releasing that tight shoe, then I wanted her to know that I understood.

We continued to talk about our trips as a family and those we took alone. The three of us had shared many wonderful times together, and now I felt that it was therapeutic to bring those times up again. Our most memorable trips were our beach adventures to both the West and East coasts. I relived those days as we talked and I'm certain she did, too.

I went on to tell her that I trusted whatever decision she made, to stay or go. I told her that only she knew now what was best. As hard as it was, I told her that if she chose to go, then I would support her. If she chose to stay, then I would fight with all my might to help her heal. Our love would endure either path.

The ICU nurses were accustomed to this sort of medical condition. Their words were comforting, and they lauded the way I spoke with my mother now. They said that family members often bicker and disagree about how long to hold on to a loved one. They argue about life-saving efforts, only looking at the situation from their own point of view.

Often a patient may be ready to let go of her physical body; but unfortunately, she is kept alive artificially to serve the needs of those left on earth. I felt better after hearing the nurses say that my willingness to let my mother go was like a breath of fresh air.

The three of us, as in life and now near death, continued to reminisce throughout the rest of the afternoon and evening. My mother only listened and squeezed my hand, while my father and I did the talking. Her heart continued to beat, but her fight armed with strong antibiotics and pain killers was nearly over. That night, we left the hospital knowing that the end was getting closer. I was worried that she would pass on and that my father and I wouldn't be there; but the nurses assured me they would call at the slightest sign of approaching death.

She Chose to Go with the Angels

I arrived home late that night, showered and fell into bed, both exhausted and sad. There was a part of me that couldn't believe my mother was dying and another part that knew her death was near.

After finally falling asleep, I woke up at 3 a.m. in a state of anxiety. It was as if the ceiling was crashing down. My heart rate was high, and my breath was shallow. That was it, I thought, she must have died! As reality hit, I jumped up and checked all the phones to see if there were any calls from the nurses. Instead of going back to sleep, I dressed and drove to the hospital.

The nurses told me that at 3 a.m., they had turned her on her side to clean the surgical incision site. She had struggled and was restless. With those words from the nurse, I knew. She had made up her mind to go. The pain was too severe to handle; the road to recovery was too much to bear, not to mention the loss of dignity and pride with her body. She had had enough. I knew. She was hanging on now, and I knew we needed to talk more before she left.

My father arrived shortly after I did that morning, well before sunrise. He, too, had awakened at exactly 3 a.m., knowing that something had changed. We both felt it, yet didn't fully understand what had happened.

Looking back, I can see that at 3 a.m. that Sunday morning, she decided to let go, unravel her cord to earth and go with the angels. Since the bond among the three of us was so strong, both my father and I had felt it, too.

Physical death can be a relatively slow process. First, the organs begin shutting down; the heart rate slows; and breaths become more shallow and spaced apart. But through this physical process, we continued to hold hands and talk about our love. By this point, she had wanted her oxygen tube off and brushed at her face and head to remove it. She was ready for her next journey, and I intuitively understood that my role had just begun in helping her find her way.

My mother and I had read various articles through the years on life's meaning, angels and other heavenly topics. We both were able to believe without seeing, had a strong faith in God and were curious about our role in the universe.

A long time ago, we had read a verse where death was described as a boat sailing off into the horizon. The boat appeared to be gone from the naked eye, but was only out of sight and off to another port. On that day in her hospital room, I held her hand and talked about that boat again. I told her how she was never going to miss a birthday, anniversary or any other celebration with me or her granddaughter. I reminded her that she will be with us, similar to the boat off the horizon, just not able to be seen with the naked eye. She softened, and I knew that she was relieved with that notion.

Our conversation continued through the morning. Even though one-sided from my father and me, we both knew that she could hear us. At one point, my father looked over at me and talked about dropping a club membership, since she would be gone. Immediately, her arms flew up as if to say, "No, keep going there to eat and drink and remember me there, too!" That was a nice confirmation that our conversations were not one-sided at all.

We talked about death being like the shedding of a snake's skin. So often on our walks in the woods, we'd see empty snake skins. Only the shell of the snake remained, but the snake left for another adventure. Just like human death, I now wondered aloud.

I felt that the three of us were not the only ones in her hospital room. As the sun streamed in the window, it was as if Heaven had crafted a ladder for her to climb out of her shell. It was magnificent, as the sunshine path was nearly blinding to my eyes. I felt my grandparents and her dear aunts and uncles had come in now, to take her hand from mine and lead her away.

I began to talk about them, her parents and their presence that I felt. I asked her to follow the light and walk with them. I noticed her brows would go up repeatedly, as if she was perhaps astonished at what she was seeing.

I imagined it was bright where she was looking, and the feeling of love was overflowing.

I even asked her about it, knowing she wouldn't be able to voice what she was seeing, but believing by the look of her brows, that it was brighter than any of our sunniest afternoons on the beach.

In the past, I'd read about the "Third Eye" (Pineal Gland) holding the gate to Heaven. I asked her to visualize that opening and trust in the love that waits on the Other Side. I didn't know where these words were coming from at the time, as they just flowed out of my mouth; but I instinctively believed I was giving her a road map for her next trip.

I continued to talk about her antiques; her mother's and grandmother's china, silver and linens; and all of the little things we never got around to organizing. I promised her that I would see to everything and look for her guidance in my intuition. I worried that she was holding on to these earthly possessions, and I wanted her to know that I would treasure the antiques and keep all the stories alive around them. I felt in my heart that it helped her to let go, knowing that everything would be handled.

I also wanted to talk to her about the notion of "time" in Heaven. It occurred to me that time is an earthly way to manage our lives while in our bodies. Surely, in Heaven, time must be an "illusion", or so I thought.

I whispered to her that in no time (Heavenly time), my father and I would be joining her. Not TOO soon, I said, to reassure myself; but in a blink of her Heavenly eye, years will pass and we'd be together again for a Heavenly reunion.

Somehow this felt right in saying, as odd as it sounded to me, yet helpful to her as she squeezed my hand tightly as I spoke. I believed the thought of us being together again helped her move to her next stage.

Around 3 p.m. that afternoon, after hours of expressing my love and thankfulness to her for being my mother, I told her that I was going to keep talking, while my father would leave to pick up lunch. The nurses were occasionally in and out checking her breathing and making sure that she was comfortable. We really didn't know at that point how long her body would take to slow down and let go. The suggestion of hospice care was mentioned by a physician; but for now, we were simply taking one hour at a time.

I told her that before my father left, I was going to step out of the room and then would come back so we could continue to talk. I left her hospital room at around 3:28 p.m. At 3:29 p.m. my mother took her last breath. My father tried to get my attention, as I walked away down the hall. But I didn't hear. I came back a few minutes later, and she was gone.

At first, I was surprised that she had chosen to die when I was out of the room. But quickly I realized that it made complete sense. She didn't want me to see her take her last breath or ever think she was gone. She wanted me to understand that while her body was gone, her Spirit was still very much alive. After the finality of the moment registered with me, I even chuckled to myself, leaned in close to her face and whispered, "I understand what you did. I would have done the same thing for my daughter. It's your final act of love!" We understood each other, and I knew she was watching now from another vantage point.

The nurses came in to confirm her death and record the official time for the Death Certificate. The sun continued to stream in her window, but now her body was completely silent and still. I visualized her walking directly into that ray of sunshine with her mother on one side, and perhaps her father on the other. I visualized her walk, looking back at me smiling and nodding, to let me know that she had made it and would be back soon, somehow, someway, to stay in touch with me.

I then began to feel almost a sense of relief, standing in the hospital room. The weight of the last five days and the months before of watching my mother in severe pain began to lift. As sad as I was to walk away, I knew that she was really okay now.

As my father and I left the hospital and walked to our cars, the dichotomy of the beautiful day and the death of my mother felt like the two most opposite extremes in the universe. I looked up at the blue sky and the birds overhead and took a deep breath of the fresh autumn air. I knew life was going to go on and a new phase of the special bond with my mother was beginning anew.

My Mother's Voice Begins

"Carve your name on hearts,
not tombstones.
A legacy is etched into the
minds of others and the stories
they share about you."

SHANNON L. ALDER

Gift to the Library

The next morning after her death, as I opened my eyes from sleep, a profound sense of grief overwhelmed me. Not only did I miss my mother more than words could describe, I knew that I needed to write the obituary and go to the funeral home with my father to make the arrangements for her visitation and burial. Thankfully, she had already specified her funeral arrangements with my father, and they had purchased two plots years ago.

My mother used to joke that she preferred the "lakefront view, under a beautiful tree". But today was different, no more joking, as those plans were now reality.

I thought long and hard about the obituary and prayed for guidance on what she would prefer, hoping for some sort of direction. Immediately, I heard a voice that whispered, "the library". Without a doubt, I knew that it was my mother's voice.

She was a voracious reader and so happy that her granddaughter had inherited that quality from her. When my daughter was a baby, my mother would read to her for hours while rocking and napping in the rocking chair. As my daughter got older, the two of them would sit in the same room, both happily buried in a book.

So, with each donation that we received at the Visitation, we would donate it to our elementary school library for more books. A perfect idea that I'm not sure I would have thought of alone.

Purple Iris

Shortly following a loved one's passing, the "business" of death is usually the first task at hand. Our business began with a meeting at the funeral home to plan the Visitation service. Sitting in the conference room with my father and listening to the instructions on how best to orchestrate my mother's event was like some sort of unsettling dream, except that I wasn't sleeping. It seemed unnatural to sit in a family meeting without my mother, even if we were discussing her grave stone, Death Certificate and the details of the Visitation.

As much as my mother had already shared her preferences with the funeral home planner years ago, there were still a few outstanding items that needed to be considered. My mother had never preferred an open casket, and now we confirmed in the meeting that her casket would be closed. On top of it, I would later select a dozen framed pictures of important events in her life. Her younger self, married self, my wedding and the birth of her beloved granddaughter, to name a few.

When the question of flowers came up, I froze in my decision-making. Now here was a detail that we'd never discussed. I closed my eyes for a split second, as I flipped through the floral book provided by the funeral home. Immediately, I heard her voice informing me to "turn the page to the purple iris arrangement".

I was stunned as I turned the page to see a beautiful array of purple (my mother's favorite color) iris, among other equally beautiful colors and stems. It was the perfect choice and most importantly, I knew we weren't alone in our decision-making. The rest of the meeting was seamless, as I knew my mother still had a voice in the details.

My Mother's Party

In the true sense of the word, "Visitation" denotes the "final visit or inspection". In our circumstance, I suppose we could have called our event, "The Final Visit with Eleanor". But then again, "visit" also implies a two-way communication.

My mother often likened the funeral home Visitation to a party, and we believed it should be a celebration versus a somber occasion. We also hoped it would be a two-way communication when that time would come.

She was there in Spirit to see how everyone from her past and present came together to celebrate her life and remember the special good times each of them enjoyed with her. At numerous times throughout the evening, I thought to myself how she would have loved this event if she were standing in her physical, pain-free body greeting everyone. She would have been proud of her granddaughter as she talked with her old friends; appreciative of my father, as he reminisced and chatted; and content knowing how supportive my husband and his family were to me.

I had picked out her favorite music to play at the event. With all the people talking and visiting, we really didn't hear the tune; but the energy of the music was there and helped convey the joyful manner in which she lived her life.

As people filed in, they slowly made their way to the casket, noting the special photos I had carefully placed on top, alongside the purple flower arrangement. So many still, yet captured, moments of love and happiness were conveyed in the pictures. Although I had only selected twelve snapshots of life, these were the ones that meant the most to her.

As I chatted with her friends and explained her physical challenges over the last few years, I was confident in my heart that she could not have "stayed" in her body any longer. It was hard for some to comprehend that notion, but those who knew her best understood.

Immediately following the Visitation, our family went to a favorite Italian restaurant for dinner in the private dining room. It was a first to be there without my mother. Yet still, we raised our glasses to toast the grand life she had led and how much we loved her. It was a bittersweet, yet memorable, evening, just as she would have planned it, I believe.

Graveside Poem

The next morning following the Visitation, my father, husband and I met at the cemetery for her private graveside service. It was a warm, beautiful October day. The casket was there, still adorned with the beautiful purple flowers that we had chosen together. At that moment in time, I knew whole-heartedly that even though her tired old body was inside that casket, she was long gone. Her Spirit was alive and well, and in a new place surrounded by love.

We had given our daughter, then a fourth grader, the choice of taking the day off from school to come to the grave or to go to school. She chose to go to school, which I supported

100%. I knew my mother would agree. She knew her grandmother was not in that casket; frankly, I wanted my daughter to remember the laughs we had shared just a few short weeks ago, instead of the finality of her casket being lowered into the ground.

We didn't plan an organized service of any sort that morning. We only each said our silent prayers as her body was "laid to rest". That is exactly the simplicity that my mother preferred.

Later that day, in continuing to keep her Spirit alive, I took some of the extra flower arrangements that guests had sent to the Visitation and gifted them to where she would have enjoyed brightening someone else's day. One green arrangement remained at our house; one was given to my daughter's elementary school library; and one brightened the hospital ICU, where she took her last breath.

My mother had saved a poem years ago that she wanted me to find and read after her death.

She had showed me the poem and where it was stored in her father's antique desk. At that time, I didn't want to think or talk about her future death. But now I knew I needed to find it again.

After the service, I went to my parent's house, found the desk and opened the drawer where I knew she had tucked it away. There were old obituaries of my grandparents and great aunts; old cards; and other items, which I decided to go through another time. Finally, I found the tiny piece of paper that had been cut out of the newspaper and clipped with a purple paper clip, my mother's favorite color.

She and I never knew who wrote that poem, but we believed it. It gave me peace in knowing that she left it for me. This time, instead of stuffing it back in the drawer, I took it home to keep.

Do not stand at my grave and weep.

I am not there, I do not sleep.

I am a thousand winds that blow.

I am the diamond glints on snow.

I am the sunlight on ripened grain.

I am the gentle autumn rain.

When you awaken in the morning's hush,

I am the swift, uplifting rush

of quiet birds in circled flight.

I am the soft stars that shine at night.

Do not stand at my grave and cry.

I am not there.

I did not die.

HER VOICE,
MY DREAMS

"Dreams say what they mean.
But they don't say it in
daytime language."

GAIL GOODWIN

My Dreams

In the first few weeks after my mother passed on, the exhaustion of both body and mind was heavy, especially the second my head hit the pillow at night. I would fall asleep immediately and never remember a single dream I'd had the night before, or if I'd even dreamed at all.

However, about three weeks after her death, my dreams began taking shape, unlike any dreams I'd ever experienced before. I began to keep pen and paper next to the bed to jot down memories I didn't want to forget. Soon I began to realize that I didn't need the paper. These dreams were unforgettable.

A respected yoga teacher once told me that dreams involving our deceased loved ones are actually "visits" from them. At the time, I wasn't too familiar with that notion; but as I began to experience it, there was no doubt my mother was visiting.

The first set of dreams after her death I named the "Healing" dreams. The images and messages I received via these dreams helped me understand that she was healed from sickness and in a place with no pain. In my dream state, we were communicating telepathically, while my conscious mind took a rest. But whether I heard her words or felt them, they were strong and consistent enough to let me know that she was now okay.

Apparently, she must have known that I understood the Healing message, because I soon began receiving actual advice that was timely for specific situations occurring in my life. I called these dreams the "Advisory" dreams, as that is exactly what they offered. A few of these dreams came at a time when I was going through her clothes and personal items, while helping my father prepare to sell their house. It was a stressful time, and I certainly could have used a dose of her wisdom and support. The other Advisory dreams offered insights that I used to help others.

In addition to Healing and Advising, there were other dreams that were simply fun and helped confirm to me that she was enjoying my life with her own new one. There was no dramatic healing or stress-reducing advice, just dream visits to help me realize that she wasn't missing out on our fun and her voice of love never died.

The last category of dreams was the most difficult to decipher. I woke up shaking my head trying to understand the message of the "Life Lesson" visits. However, once I opened my heart and suspended judgment, the meanings became clear.

Sedona Healing

DREAM

In this dream, we were walking together to a field near a beautiful vista of red rocks to find a perfect spot for viewing an air show. I didn't recognize the other people around us and noted to myself how no one was noticing us. Each person was simply walking and getting ready for the show.

We didn't seem to care about the others, rather only focusing on the two of us. As we sat down, I looked up thinking that this place looked just like Sedona, Arizona. Sedona was a spot where my mother and I had spent a wonderful Mother's Day a few years back, and we fell in love with the beauty of the landscape and energy there.

Near the spot where we sat, there was a large adobe style home on the side of the red rocks with the most amazing roof I had ever seen. The roof was a shade of deep purple, similar to the highest crown chakra color; and the house appeared as a highly charged beacon on the hill with a powerful light. I had never seen anything more beautiful in such a wondrous colorful setting.

Next, we sat down together to watch the air show. It was no surprise that she had taken me to an air show, as airplanes and jet travel had always been an important part of our lives. My father had worked for years at TWA; and as a family, we had loved to travel and attend air shows together.

In this dream, she was wearing the cream-colored sweatshirt that I had bought her for her birthday some twenty years earlier. This shirt had been a favorite of hers for many years. But the most important and memorable part of the dream was when she reached out to hold my hands and show me her hands and lower arms. She said, "Look Lisa, the (IV) scars have healed! I AM HEALED!"

Her hands looked beautiful and young. There was new smooth skin where the IV's used to be. There were no brown spots or bony arthritic protrusions on the joints. It was a miracle.

We continued to sit and watch the air show together; and I felt such a miraculous sense of peace, knowing that she was no longer in pain. As the planes darted in and out, I noticed that the sky changed to dark grey as the clouds were moving incredibly fast directly above us.

Suddenly, one of the planes took a nose dive straight into the canyon, and I woke up abruptly. As quickly as I woke up, I immediately knew that my mother was healed. Not only were her hands healed, but also the new fresh, pink skin was a sign of her new beginning. The plane may have crashed in the canyon, but the show was still going on.

Aerobics in Heaven

DREAM

In my late 20s and early 30s, I lived and worked in Chicago. When I'd come home to visit my parents, my mother loved taking me to her aerobics class at the wellness center at her local hospital. It was a great chance for her friends there to meet me, her only daughter whom she'd talked about for years. We used to joke that it was more social than aerobic; but I knew that it made her happy for me to join her, so I did.

In this "aerobics" dream, I distinctly remember her taking me to her "new" class. Who knows if there are exercise classes in Heaven; but if there are, I know for a fact, that my mother is leading the class!

In this dream, we were walking through a crowded room of people waiting for the class to begin. We stood in line together, and the woman at the check-in desk glanced up at me and asked where I was from.

I replied, "EARTH", and the whole class, including my mother and me, burst into laughter!

This vision was yet another healing confirmation for me. My mother was now exercising, healed and out of pain, bringing me to her class once again. Aerobics healing in Heaven was my message from her, loud and clear.

Seventeen Steps

DREAM

As my mother's back pain worsened during her life, there were seventeen challenging steps to climb, or in the end, nearly crawl, up to her bedroom. But in this dream, I was giving a friend of mine a tour of their home. We stopped at the bottom of the steps, and I began to demonstrate how difficult it was for my mother to make it upstairs every night. I recalled to my friend how unhappy this made me feel for her, as I knew that she loved her house so much.

Suddenly, I looked up and saw my mother standing at the top of the stairs, smiling ear to ear and waving! For a split second, I said to myself, "Oh, you aren't dead after all. You must have recovered from the infection!"

She nodded in agreement that YES, she had recovered, and now the steps were not a problem at all!

Indeed, she did recover. I heard her say that in Heaven the steps are never challenging, the pain never starts and the love never forgets.

Smooth Ride

DREAM

A year after my mother's death, my father was preparing to sell their home and move to a new smaller house, where old friends lived across the street in a familiar neighborhood.

Immediately after the real estate deal was finalized, my mother visited via another dream. This time, the three of us were on a plane traveling to a new destination. While we were generally happy about the trip ahead, I was a bit nervous about the new destination.

I was walking up and down the cabin in the airplane, checking seat assignments and timetables. My father was an involved passenger on the plane, talking to the crew and looking forward to the new journey. But most importantly, there was my mother, sitting in a seat watching us and assuring me that the move would be a good one.

After I woke up and reflected, I realized that my desire to check everything on the plane was a metaphor for the work that I was helping my father with in his new home. Now that I knew that my mother was on board, I was relieved to know that we were in for a smooth ride ahead.

New Home Remodel

Understandably, when it came to paint colors and carpet selections for the new home, my father was going to need some help. In the past, these decisions would have been made completely by my mother. Now, I was happy to step in and help him create a beautiful new home without the redecorating worries.

I soon became immersed in the details of trim, paint, what to remodel, what to keep and what could be finished before his actual move-in date. As I tried to perfect the details, another powerful and very detailed dream provided the support that I needed to let me know that yet again, my mother was by my side.

In this dream, I was at my father's house, waiting to meet the painter to discuss paint colors for his new home. As I opened the door to let the painter in, I noticed my mother sitting on the sofa. She smiled at me softly and nodded her head to approve the process at hand and my involvement in the details. She looked like she did at around 40 years of age, with no wrinkles and natural-colored hair. She was wearing white summer pants and her favorite turquoise-colored sweater, that she often wore on summer nights to dinner or on vacation to warmer spots. Her outfit reminded me of good times spent together at the beach or lake.

In my dream, I asked myself how she could be wearing that sweater now, since I had donated it just a few weeks ago. As I was going through her closets, I distinctly recalled holding it up, remembering the good dinners and laughs we'd shared when she last had it on. She must have remembered, too.

She then began to tell me about the painter, and emphatically told me not to worry about his schedule, as she was sure he would begin work prior to my father moving in. Even more specifically, she told me that the painter would meet with us on Saturday, October 27th (2012), when everyone would have more time to review all the details in person. In my dream, I questioned her date, since we already had a date set to meet with the painter three days earlier. She pressed on and told me that everything would be handled.

When I woke up, I made note of the date that she had mentioned, for future reference. I was still shocked at the details and dates that she had conveyed to me. That afternoon, the painter called to cancel our first meeting date and reschedule for October 27th, when he would have more time to go over all the specifics of the job.

In the same dream, after she shared painting specifics, I recalled that my mother and I went out for ice cream to talk about the remodel. I was sitting at a table with my mother and noticed an old friend in line with her parents. More specifically, this was the same friend that had provided much needed guidance to me on the new carpet selection just the other day.

I was telling my mother about the carpet details in the new house, while my friend looked at me from across the room, mouthing to say, "How can your mother be here getting ice cream? I was at her Visitation…"

I looked back, shrugging my shoulders and said, "I know, it's hard to believe; but she's definitely here now," as my mother smiled and nodded in agreement.

After I woke up, I knew that she was definitely here now with me, whenever I needed her. This dream provided even more evidence to believe that love never dies and continues on to help via Spirit. I thanked my mother for that reassurance and guidance.

Song List

DREAM

Ａs I was beginning to weed through my mother's possessions, I was also in the midst of co-chairing a major fundraiser in our hometown. The event was coming up in less than two weeks. But the beverage donation was still uncertain, and I was waiting to hear a confirmation on song specifics from the entertainer.

Knowing that my stress level was high, my mother shared her advice to me in a dream. We were at the event, and she was wearing the beautiful outfit that she wore to my wedding. She walked up to me; handed me the entertainer's song list for the evening; confirmed that the beverage donation was being handled; and asked me to make sure that my daughter would be able to meet the entertainer prior to the show. And, as a truly practical mother, she showed me the outfit that I would be wearing, one that was already hanging in my closet.

I woke up with renewed confidence surrounding the event and knew for a fact that I had another helper behind the scenes. The night of the event, I wore the plum-colored dress that she had suggested and happily watched my daughter treasure a special autograph. I listened as the songs on the list that she handed me were played and enjoyed by the audience, and watched as the libations were poured.

Standing backstage, I delightedly watched the evening unfold. I happened to look down at her wedding ring on my hand, nestled with my rings now, as it glistened and shone.

Interestingly enough, even a member of the band standing next to me backstage commented about the bright light shining from my rings. Indeed, the light of love was shining on a successful evening, with more help than anyone would have ever imagined.

Lowe's

DREAM

In another Advising dream, my mother must have known that I was concerned about the many errands and new home chores my father was now facing in his new home. His neighborhood Lowe's store was just a few blocks away, and that's what I named this dream.

In the "Lowe's" dream, she explained that in order for me to better understand things, we needed to look at them from a "higher level or perspective". Suddenly, she took me to a place where we were watching my father from a high vantage point. We were sitting at a nice little sidewalk café, but the view looking down was incredible. I remembered thinking to myself how unusual it was to sit at a café so high up!

Immediately, I realized what she wanted me to see. I watched my father as he was running errands, going back and forth to Lowe's and picking up various items for his new house. Never sitting down, never resting, we both watched him always on the go.

My mother then said, "This is what your father likes to do… accomplish tasks and get things done!" And incidentally, she added, "There is absolutely NOTHING you can do to help him, as he prefers to work alone!"

Bill's Welcome

DREAM

After I heard my mother describe how my deceased grandmother (her mother) visited her in the hospital, I was convinced that we're not alone moving to the next stage of life. I'd read that when we pass on, our loved ones stand waiting on the "Other Side" for our arrival. Family, friends and even pets all gather round for the official greeting ceremony. While this scene filled me with peace, I often wondered if it could really be a possibility.

After a dear family friend had passed on, my mother offered me a glimpse into this ceremony. Our friend had lived an adventurous, full life.

His wife and he had shared years of wonderful memories with my parents. Sadly, in his later years, Alzheimer's disease had robbed him of most of these memories.

The night after his passing, I dreamed that my mother had taken me to a beautiful, delicious seafood buffet. Together, we laughed about the biggest shrimp we'd ever seen and the most perfect lobster tails and crab legs that only a true seafood connoisseur could truly adore. I asked her what was going on. Is there a special celebration?

Her reply was simple, yet timely. "Bill's here now."

I knew without a doubt in that early waking hour that this must be Bill's Heavenly Welcome Party.

Choir

DREAM

Before my mother passed on, I often asked for her opinion about topics surrounding parenting and school, since she and her granddaughter were so close. Now, as my daughter was planning for middle school and weighing class options, I knew that my mother would have enjoyed sharing her thoughts.

We had been talking about the notion of taking the Choir elective, along with a full year of Orchestra, since my daughter played the cello. Clearly my mother had an opinion on this topic; when I woke up, I vividly remembered her dream visit.

In the dream, she came to me and handed me a piece of paper. As I looked at the paper, I recalled thinking what a pleasure it was to see my mother's handwriting again. There, big and large on the page it said, "CHOIR!"

Broadway Musicals

Dream visits can also occur without Healing or Advising messages. Instead, the takeaway is that our loved ones are enjoying our lives right along with us.

I'll never forget the summer after my mother passed on, when my daughter and I rented nearly every Broadway musical from the 1940s and 1950s. We loved watching the old classics that she must have also enjoyed when she was young.

My mother's Grand Piano now sits in our living room, along with her sheet music from the 1940s. One night, after watching "South Pacific," I had a wonderful dream where my mother was in our living room, playing her Grand Piano. She was playing and singing all the way through the music. It was truly joyous watching her in my dream, and I believed that she must have been enjoying all the old musicals right along with us that summer.

Essence

I was the student in this Life Lesson dream, in which my mother and I chatted while sitting around a small table. She explained her "essence" by saying that when she left her physical body in the hospital, she entered a new level of "being".

Her Spirit, as she called it, could go anywhere at any time without any physical or time constraints. As she left her body, her essence could spread. Similar to when a bottle of perfume is opened, she said, the smell travels out of the bottle into the atmosphere. She was now explaining that the same notion holds true in physical death and rebirth.

Her essence could travel and be a resource for healing. Any sort of healing, she emphasized, such as emotional or physical. She compared this idea to a car that requires gas to move. Her car or physical body was gone, so she didn't need any gas to live. However, for us in the physical world, we still require the gas. If we need an extra boost or healing (physical or emotional), she could fill me with her essence. All I needed to do was ask.

This was a lofty concept and still difficult to understand, but she pressed on in the dream. She showed me a purple, hazy fog that was floating between the two of us. I waved my arms in it to take in as much as I could. This, she said, was her essence for me to absorb.

My lesson from this dream was this: Our loved ones can continue to spread their essence, their truest qualities, if only we ask.

Death is Just Another Part of Life

DREAM

Since music played a big role in my mother's life on Earth, it makes sense that it might be a big part of her new life, too. Indeed, in another piano performance dream, I watched my mother laughing, singing and performing with another pianist on a stage.

She was having a fabulous time; and after the show, I walked backstage to congratulate her.

She was wearing her typical summer attire, white pants and a coral v-neck sweater. I noticed how relaxed she seemed, as she took my hand and led me to a nearby boat dock. I could only see the backs of the boats, sitting peacefully and bobbing on a perfect blue bay, as the sun was beginning to set.

Amid this gorgeous setting, I had the uneasy feeling that she was going somewhere on one of the boats. She then reached out to hug me tightly. I remember thinking, if only we could hug like this again.

"But we are," she said, as she read my mind, "Death is just another part of Life."

She told me again how much she loved me, and I knew for a fact that love never dies. She said she'd see me again soon and turned to walk away. As she walked to her boat ride, I waved good-bye, for now.

HER VOICE, MY SIGNS

"The living owe it to those who no longer can speak to tell their story for them."

CZESLAW MILOSZ

My Signs

I discovered that as I became more open to Spirit, the Signs from my mother were everywhere to see. On some days, the Signs have been clearer than on others. I'm certain that on many occasions, there have been Signs that I have never even noticed. But on the days that I did notice the Signs, I continued to be in awe of Spirit and the meanings behind each Sign that I was fortunate enough to understand.

The Signs always had messages that were particularly relevant for whatever I was experiencing at the time. It's as if Spirit has its own special language that we all can see and hear, if only we make the conscious choice to open our eyes and ears.

Signs can appear in a variety of ways, some being very subtle while others are much more dramatic. My personal examples have included unexplained coincidences in the form of radio songs; cloud shapes; license plates; unexpected, yet perfectly timed, calls from a friend; and even unusual bird visits.

I began to understand that our loved ones all have the ability to arrange synchronicity to let us know that we are never alone and that they are okay. Most importantly, this synchronicity tells us that love never forgets and love never dies.

Gifts from the Radio

I'd heard about the notion of specific radio songs being heard as special gifts from Spirit. But after my mother passed away, a song was no longer "just" a song. Here's why:

As I was writing the obituary on the morning after my mother's death, my daughter turned on the radio to hear our first Sign via a song. That morning, Radio Disney was playing preschool songs, versus the older kid songs that she usually enjoyed. As soon as she turned on the radio, a voice sang loud and clear: "I'm so proud of you!"

Although a common phrase, of course, these were the words that my mother would say to her granddaughter EVERY time they were together. Without a doubt, my daughter and I believed that my mother had found a way to tell my daughter, yet again, how proud she was of her and will always be.

Another radio gift occurred on the last day of my daughter's fourth grade school year, the same year my mother passed on. We were going out to dinner to celebrate the school year's end, letting our daughter invite a friend and pick the restaurant. She chose a favorite Mexican spot, and we celebrated the now fifth graders. My father joined the four of us; although unsaid at the time, I felt that the only thing missing was my mother, raising her glass and enjoying the tamales and tacos alongside the rest of us.

As soon as we ordered, my mother's favorite song came over the sound system, "Celebration" by Kool and the Gang. I smiled, not stopping to explain my delight to anyone, yet knowing wholeheartedly, that this was her way of letting me know that she was truly a part of the evening. She loved that song and had danced to it on so many special occasions. If she were to pick a song for us to hear when we were celebrating, that would be it. I also remembered her telling me that in the days when her mother was near death, she would drive away from the nursing home, put in the "Celebration" tape and try to feel better by remembering the good times spent with HER mother.

Later that evening, I was telling my daughter how proud I was of her outstanding grades and accomplishments over the last year. Then I told her that I also knew that her grandmother would be SO proud, too. That's when she said, "Oh, I know Mom, I heard her favorite song tonight at the restaurant, I bet she was there, too!" Yes, we were all celebrating together with the right song at the right time.

Lesson in the Musical

SIGNS

The first Christmas after my mother passed on, everything in our Christmas decorations, food and holiday traditions reminded me of her. As was tradition over the past few years, my mother, along with my daughter and me, would attend an annual Christmas Program full of carols, the Christmas Story and orchestra music. This year, my daughter and I attended the program by ourselves. Sitting in the audience without her, I longed for her physical presence.

This year, the story was centered on a girl who had just lost her mother. Her sadness was captured in her mannerisms, as the other characters sang and danced to the spirit of the season. The girl received support from her family and friends, but her pain was never really eased. As the musical progressed and her heart opened, she began to see her mother in her dreams. Slowly her pain began to fade, and she was able to truly experience the love of the Christmas season again.

It touched my heart when the girl onstage lay dreaming, as her mother, dressed in white, appeared and sang as angels danced nearby. My daughter and I both felt the magic and knew that my mother, her grandmother, was near helping us understand how death is just another way of being, and that the veil that separates us is thin. I couldn't help but feel that my mother was with us that afternoon and perhaps had a hand in crafting that special message for us to see.

Miracle on my Laptop Screen

SIGNS

Several months after my mother passed on, I experienced what I could only describe as a miracle on my laptop screen.

I had wrapped up some work on my laptop at home and logged off from my email account. Leaving my desk area, I walked back to the bedroom, stopping to gaze at a framed photo of my parents from my wedding. Suddenly, I heard a voice in my head nudging me to go back to my computer for a message. At the time, I wasn't sure if that inner voice was my intuition or my mother, but the thought, nonetheless, was loud and clear. Although I questioned myself and asked silently how there could be a message on my computer, curiosity got the best of me. I stopped what I was doing and headed back to my desk.

I had left my computer on, so after closing my email account, the only visual on my screen was a picture of my family from a recent vacation. Around the photo sat the various desktop icons and files I'd kept on my screen. As I walked into the room and glanced at my laptop, the screen was dramatically different.

On my laptop screen, an Amazon shopping website featuring a specific book stared back at me! Immediately, I called to the other room to see if my husband had been shopping on Amazon. His answer? A resounding "No!" I asked my daughter, who had never shopped on Amazon before. Again, another strong, "No!"

A book was displayed on the screen, titled *Downward Dog, Upward Fog*. I had never heard of this book, which was a first novel for the author. As I read the description of the main character, I couldn't help but identify with her. Although she was younger than I am, with no children, her spiritual adventures caught my eye. The back cover read, "A rare gem: women's fiction for spiritual seekers." This is a book my mother would have enjoyed, and now she was recommending it to me!

Downward Dog, Upward Fog
A Novel by Meryl Davids Landau
Publication Date: May 3, 2011

Description on the back cover:
"Lorna Crawford's (main character) seeking is put to the ultimate test when personal tragedy strikes. Will she come to truly understand that living spiritually has little to do with how you pretzel yourself on the yoga mat (although she gets plenty good at that), and everything to do with embracing the twists in everyday life?"

Without a doubt, I ordered the book. That night, I continued to search for some physical explanation for what had occurred. It seemed as if it was impossible for that book to have appeared on my screen. I had not shopped on Amazon, and no one with access to my computer had ever heard of the book or author before. There was another force at hand I couldn't see or fully understand. This was truly remarkable and a viable Sign from my mother.

After reading the book, I understood why she had recommended it. Here was the main character, struggling with her own spirituality in light of a crisis and finally beginning to open her heart to the unknown. None of the self-help spiritual books she'd read in the past had shifted her in this direction. The character, similar to me, was learning to trust in Spirit and believe wholeheartedly in what is not seen.

Flowering Quince

SIGNS

After my father had some routine surgery, a year after my mother had passed on, I was caught off guard when visiting him in his hospital room for the first time. He was in the same hospital where my mother had become so ill, and those memories became incredibly vivid the second I stepped off the elevator. It was as if time had stood still.

Even the ride up the elevator to see my father felt the same as it had a year earlier to see my mother. As I walked around the corner to his room, I realized that it seemed to be identical to the one that my mother had been in, before her final weekend in the Intensive Care Unit. I knew that I'd never forget that room, and indeed, now it seemed as if it was just yesterday that we were there together.

Suddenly, I was reliving the moments when I had stood in this very same spot and was pacing back and forth, calling her friends, my friends and my husband, as my mother lay nearby, slowly leaving her body. Now, here I was again, and I couldn't help but replay the past in my mind.

After I knew that my father was stable that day, I went home for a few minutes. Secretly, I was hoping for a Sign from my mother that she was somehow involved that day with his recovery.

The minute I walked in my house, the phone rang. It was a dear college friend from Memphis, who also had loved my mother. She had called to tell me that she was driving home and couldn't help but notice the Flowering Quinces blooming everywhere. As she saw those buds in bloom, she'd had an urgent thought to call me right away. My friend also said that my mother had told her that the Flowering Quinces always bloom for their birthdays, both in April. So, as she was driving through Memphis on that glorious spring day, all she could think about was my mother.

We chatted for quite some time, caught up on our lives, and shared other news. She understood the pain of losing a parent, as both her parents had now passed on, and talking to her that afternoon was a remedy for me to feel grounded again.

Later, as I understood that there are no coincidences, I could look back and know that my good friend saw the Flowering Quinces and thought of her friend (my mother) and my loss, at exactly the right time I needed to hear her story. Her call was no accident, and my mother knew that a friendly voice and a special story were the perfect antidote to help heal a sad memory.

Clouds Take Heart

SIGNS

The summer after my mother passed on, I would often run into old friends and acquaintances that had not heard our news. On a particularly warm evening after running errands with my family, we stopped at our favorite frozen yogurt shop on the way home. Nothing beats a cold sweet treat on a hot summer night, and we all settled into our favorite chairs and chatted about the day.

As we ate, a woman who had taken aerobics with my mother years ago came in with her kids. After I moved away, my mother would tell me about the girls in her class who were close in age to me that she had befriended and often advised on their life issues. Especially in my absence, it was a blessing for both my mother and her new young friends.

As we chatted, I knew that this former classmate of my mother's had no idea that my mother had died. She did ask, "So how is your mom doing these days?" I told her the short version of the back surgery, the MRSA infection, and the final few days in the hospital. I hadn't spoken her story for awhile; although nine months had passed, the words didn't come easy.

Later, as we were driving home, the sun was setting in one of the most beautiful sunsets I had seen in some time. I told my husband and daughter that it seemed as though the ocean should be sitting underneath that huge orange ball. As we all looked to the north, the most beautiful, yet odd, cloud formation began to form. My husband commented for all of us to look up.

Two clouds had pushed together leaving a giant blue sky hole in the middle. The hole was in the shape of a beautiful heart! I felt strongly that at that very moment, this was my mother's way of making her presence known. I had just had a very difficult conversation about my mother's death, and it was exactly nine months to the day of her rebirth. (October 2 to July 2)

That amazing heart in the sky said to me, "I love you." I knew then, as always, that our hearts were forever connected.

Butterflies on the Path

SIGNS

Exactly one year after my mother passed on, I took a long walk on the path and trails we walked together. I'd found in the last year that mindful walking was a form of meditation for me. I could close the clutter of my mind and get in touch with nature. On this special day, a beautiful blue sky, a calm wind and the leaves of autumn gently fell around the trail.

Unlike how I felt on the days before her passing, today I felt the heavy pain of loss. I asked for a Sign, some little miracle of nature to show me that my mother was near. Nothing happened but the fall of a single tear down my cheek, as I worked hard to maintain my workout. Then suddenly, a few yellow and white butterflies flocked around me as I walked. After another minute or so, more little creatures joined. Soon I had what I would call an entire swarm of butterflies darting back and forth across my path, both in front of me and behind.

I was certain this was more than a coincidence of butterfly nature, as I had never seen such a large group of butterflies together, nor witnessed them flying with me for such a long time! It was such a funny sight that at one point, I even laughed out loud at the oddity of my flying companions.

I remembered my mother explaining that after my grandfather (her father) passed on, she would often see little white butterflies around her, especially when her thoughts were grieving him. With that notion in mind, I was convinced that this was my Sign from my mother. I was meant to remember what she told me about her father, so that I would see her Sign for me, 365 days after her last breath.

Blue Cat Pin

Although I has received many Signs and Dreams from my mother, I had yet to see an inanimate object move in any of them. However, as I continued to believe in the power of Spirit, I realized that nothing is impossible.

My mother had cherished a blue cat pin that we had bought together at the Art Institute of Chicago. She loved her Chicago trips to visit me when I lived there, and the pin was a symbol of the fun visits we shared together. She kept the pin in her bathroom, in a jewelry holder that my daughter had made for her.

As my father was preparing to remodel the bathroom prior to selling their house, we'd purchased new faucets and left the boxes on the floor for the plumber to install at a later date. The morning after we'd stacked the boxes in the bathroom, my father happened to glance in the room and was startled to see her beloved cat pin poised on top of the faucet boxes!

No one had been in that bathroom, since we had placed the boxes there the day before. Without a doubt, I knew that she was on board with the remodel and still very much a part of the house decision-making.

License Plates

SEDONA

Sometimes the simplest of things can be the most revealing, when it comes to receiving Signs from our loved ones. I'd never given much significance to license plates in my life. In fact, I'd hardly noticed any plates, except for the one on my own car. But as I started seeing "coincidental" plates that had significant meanings for me, I knew that they were more than random numbers and letters.

On my favorite walk, there's a bridge where I often acknowledged my mother's presence. This was the bridge we had walked on together and the exact spot where I had shared important happenings in my life. We discussed career changes, boyfriend updates, marriage plans and even my dreams of motherhood. She always listened with openness, without judgment and always with unconditional love. On that day, I longed for her physical presence to share the highs and lows of my life now.

I stopped on the bridge and happened to look down. At that moment, a pebble had landed in the middle of the water. The rings circled out, again and again until the entire width of the creek was one big circle with several small ones inside. I was reminded how one splash, or one thought, can create ripples of energy to everyone near, whether in physical or Spirit form. With that notion, I hoped my desire for a Sign would reach her.

I smiled and continued to walk. As I crossed the street, a car turned in front of me with a personalized license plate. It said SEDONA on the front and rear. Sedona, Arizona was our favorite destination for hiking and reflection together. Seeing that personalized plate at that very moment took me back to the time we had spent there and gave me the feeling of her presence once again.

EK

Another license plate phenomenon occurred on an evening where my daughter and I had planned a holiday celebration, just for the two of us. In the past, we would have invited my mother along, since this was the kind of evening she'd enjoy, too. We treated ourselves to a nice Italian dinner and then a special holiday musical program.

Driving home, I began to notice the license plates of the cars in front of us and to our sides. For a solid mile or so, nearly every plate had the initials EK.

EK, my mother's initials, were everywhere for us to see. Random license plates, perhaps; but then again, quite possibly a Sign that she had enjoyed our girl's night as well.

MOM

I'd often steal away, in between carpooling my daughter and her friends around town, to a local coffee spot to write. One night during a long basketball practice, I was looking forward to two hours of uninterrupted time to reflect.

As I parked my car, I couldn't help but chuckle as the car next to me had the perfect personalized license plate for my evening of writing about my mother. It said, simply, MOM, and I knew that I wasn't alone.

Birthday Blue Jay

My mother had a particular fondness for birds, especially the blue jay. Despite their cries versus songs, she was inclined to feed them on a daily basis. When my daughter was a toddler, we often joined my mother for lunch; according to my daughter, I could never duplicate the grilled cheese sandwiches she had at her grandmother's house.

Since my daughter never liked the bread crust, the blue jays would get a special treat of grilled cheese crust. After several months, one blue jay would wait in the trees around lunch time; when the crust was thrown out, he'd swoop in for the leftovers!

For some reason, at my house, several robins, sparrows and cardinals were frequent visitors but we never saw any blue jays until one special occasion.

The occasion was my mother's birthday, a few years after she had passed on. I was hoping for a Sign from her that day. We had both loved our birthdays; even though I couldn't see her, I still celebrated her special day in my heart.

The Sign came as I was standing in the kitchen making breakfast and heard a knocking sound at the kitchen window. I walked closer to see where the noise was coming from and there, a big blue jay was knocking on the window, as if he was trying to get my attention!

I laughed at his perfect timing and knew it had to be more than a coincidence. The next day, as I heard the blue jay call, I looked out to see a bird nest that I hadn't seen before. As I looked closer, three tiny blue jay beaks were waiting for their mother to come home.

I felt then that I'd received a birthday gift, a special nest of blue jays to call our home, their home, now.

One More Blue Jay Sign:
A NEST FOR YOU

In truth,
the Birthday Blue Jay
"nest-building"
mirrors this new nest
that I am building from
the Spirit world
to you on Earth.
Please continue your
exploration at
youaremyvoice.com.